LANGUAGE ARTS

EXPLORER JUNIOR

How to Write an Interview

by Cecilia Minden
and Kate Roth

CHERRY LAKE PUBLISHING · ANN ARBOR, MICHIGAN

Published in the United States of America by Cherry Lake Publishing
Ann Arbor, Michigan
www.cherrylakepublishing.com

Content Adviser: Jeannette Mancilla-Martinez, EdD, Assistant Professor of
Literacy, Language, and Culture, University of Illinois at Chicago

Design and Illustration: The Design Lab

Photo Credits: Page 4, ©iStockphoto.com/Maica; page 6, ©iStockphoto.
com/stuartbur; page 10, ©iofoto/Shutterstock, Inc.

Library of Congress Cataloging-in-Publication Data
Minden, Cecilia.
  How to write an interview/by Cecilia Minden and Kate Roth.
     p. cm.—(Language arts explorer junior)
  Includes bibliographical references and index.
  ISBN-13: 978-1-60279-996-7 (lib. bdg.)
  ISBN-10: 1-60279-996-2 (lib. bdg.)
  1. Interviewing in journalism—Juvenile literature. I. Roth, Kate. II.
Title. III. Series.
  PN4784.I6M45 2011
  070.4'3—dc22   2010029824

Cherry Lake Publishing would like to acknowledge the work
of The Partnership for 21st Century Skills. Please visit
www.21stcenturyskills.org for more information.

Printed in the United States of America
Corporate Graphics Inc.
January 2011
CLSP08

Table of Contents

CHAPTER ONE

The Interview

You can learn a lot about someone by asking questions.

How can you learn about other people? You can do an **interview**. You might discover something new about someone you already know!

An interview is a meeting. One person asks another person questions. The answers can be written up for other people to read. How do you write an interview? First, you choose someone to interview. Then you follow these basic steps:

1. Decide what you already know.
2. Decide what you want to know.
3. Interview the person.
4. Use your notes to write up the interview.

For your first interview, pick someone you know. Maybe there is a classmate you would like to know better. In this book, we'll create an example interview with a new student.

Here's what you'll need to complete the activities in this book:

- Notebook
- Pen
- Ruler
- **Recorder**

CHAPTER TWO

Do Your Research!

Do some **research** before the interview. The student in our example is from Toronto, Canada. Learn about that city first. What you learn may give you ideas for good questions.

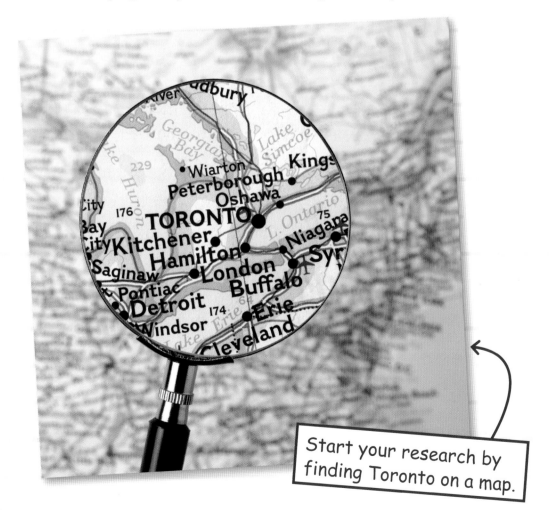

Start your research by finding Toronto on a map.

What comes to your mind when you think about Canada?

As you prepare, use a chart to keep track of what you already know. This may lead you to more questions. Let's say you know that the new student plays soccer. Does he play other sports? You know he likes animals. Does he have pets?

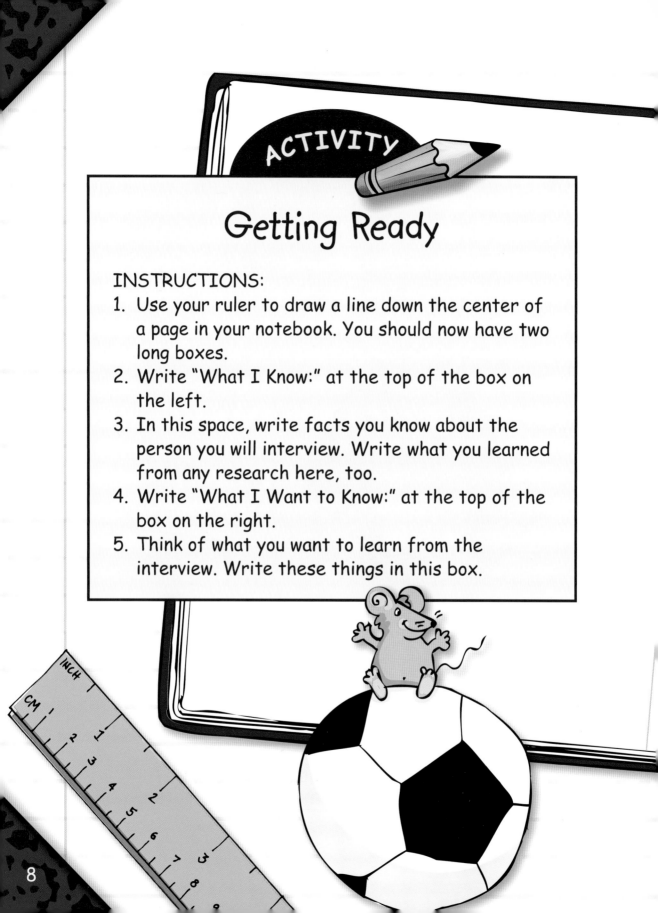

Getting Ready

INSTRUCTIONS:
1. Use your ruler to draw a line down the center of a page in your notebook. You should now have two long boxes.
2. Write "What I Know:" at the top of the box on the left.
3. In this space, write facts you know about the person you will interview. Write what you learned from any research here, too.
4. Write "What I Want to Know:" at the top of the box on the right.
5. Think of what you want to learn from the interview. Write these things in this box.

WHAT I KNOW:	WHAT I WANT TO KNOW:
• His name is Dominic.	• If he has pets
• He likes animals.	• What he liked to do in Toronto
• He is on the soccer team.	• Did he play hockey in Toronto?
• He is from Toronto, Canada.	• What he misses about living there
• Hockey is a popular sport in Canada.	

CHAPTER THREE

Write Great Questions

Writing good questions is an important part of getting ready to interview someone.

Think of questions you will ask during the interview. Start with questions that have a yes or no answer. They are easier to answer. For example, you can ask, "Do you like to play soccer?" The person will answer "yes" or "no."

You will also want to ask questions that will give you more information. For example, the question "Why is soccer your favorite sport?" lets the person give an **opinion**. The person may share his reasons for liking soccer.

It is important to have a list of questions ready before the interview. Pay attention to the speaker's answers. They can help you think of even more questions to ask.

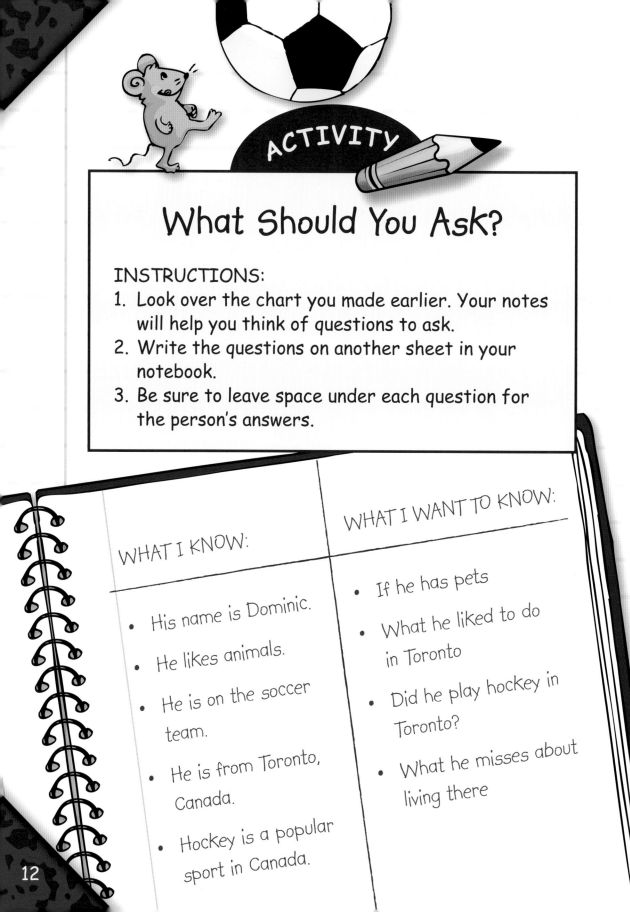

What Should You Ask?

INSTRUCTIONS:
1. Look over the chart you made earlier. Your notes will help you think of questions to ask.
2. Write the questions on another sheet in your notebook.
3. Be sure to leave space under each question for the person's answers.

WHAT I KNOW:

- His name is Dominic.
- He likes animals.
- He is on the soccer team.
- He is from Toronto, Canada.
- Hockey is a popular sport in Canada.

WHAT I WANT TO KNOW:

- If he has pets
- What he liked to do in Toronto
- Did he play hockey in Toronto?
- What he misses about living there

QUESTIONS:

Q: When did you move here?
A:

Q: I learned that hockey is popular in Canada. Do you play?
A:

Q: What did you like to do in Toronto?
A:

Q: What do you miss about Toronto?
A:

Q: Do you have any pets? If so, what kind?
A:

Q: Would you like to say anything else?
A:

CHAPTER FOUR

Be a Good Listener

Now it is time for the interview! It is a good idea to use a recorder during the interview. You can play the interview back later. It will help you remember details. Ask the interviewee for permission before recording the interview.

It is a good idea to use a recorder during an interview.

Interviewing someone can be a lot of fun!

ACTIVITY

Conducting the Interview

INSTRUCTIONS:
1. Turn on the recorder if you are using one. Don't forget to turn it off after the interview.
2. Ask the questions on your list. Give the speaker time to answer each one.

(CONTINUED ON PAGE 16)

ACTIVITY

(CONDUCTING THE INTERVIEW CONTINUED)

3. Listen carefully. Take notes on what you want to remember about each answer. Your notes do not have to be full sentences, but they should be clear. Are you planning on using a person's exact words in part of your report? Be sure to write down those words exactly as they were spoken.

4. Look at the speaker as you take notes.

5. After the interview, thank the person for taking the time to talk with you.

Thank you for taking the time to talk with me!

QUESTIONS:

Q: When did you move here?
A: 3 months ago

Q: I learned that hockey is popular in Canada.
   Do you play?
A: Yes—one of my favorite sports

Q: What did you like to do in Toronto?
A: Going to zoo ←

This answer could lead you to ask, "What is your favorite animal?"

Q: What do you miss about Toronto?
A: My friends

Q: Do you have any pets? If so, what kind?
A: Yes—cat named Chip

Q: Would you like to say anything else?
A: Like it here. Will visit Toronto this summer.

Make Choices

Read your notes. Decide what to write in the interview. You don't have to use everything from your notes. Stick with the most interesting points.

ACTIVITY

Writing the Interview

INSTRUCTIONS:
1. Choose the information you want to use from your notes. Put this information into **paragraphs**.
2. Write the interview on another page in your notebook. Imagine you are writing the interview for your classmates to read.
3. Begin by giving the person's name.
4. Write a new paragraph for each **topic**.

AN INTERVIEW WITH OAK ELEMENTARY'S NEWEST STUDENT

There's a new boy at our school. His name is Dominic. He moved here 3 months ago from Toronto, Canada.

Dominic plays soccer. It is one of his favorite sports. He also likes playing hockey.

He liked visiting the zoo in Toronto. That's not surprising because he loves animals. He has a cat named Chip.

Dominic likes it here, but he misses his friends in Toronto.

Say hi when you see Dominic in the halls. Let's all make him feel welcome!

Final Touches

Make your interview report more interesting by adding **quotes**. When you quote someone, you must write exactly what the speaker said. Put quotation marks around the person's exact words.

Quotes

INSTRUCTIONS:
1. Read your interview report.
2. Replay the interview if you used a recorder. Listen for interesting quotes. Make sure you use the person's exact words.
3. Add any quotes to your report using quotation marks.

AN INTERVIEW WITH OAK ELEMENTARY'S NEWEST STUDENT

There's a new boy at our school. His name is Dominic. He moved here 3 months ago from Toronto, Canada.

Dominic plays soccer. It is one of his favorite sports. He also likes playing hockey.

He liked visiting the zoo in Toronto. That's not surprising because he loves animals. He has a cat named Chip.

Dominic likes it here, but he misses his friends in Toronto. "It's not easy being the new kid in class. Making friends can be hard," he says.

Say hi when you see Dominic in the halls. Let's all make him feel welcome!

After you finish writing, go over your work. Make changes until everything is just right. Then give the person you interviewed a copy of your writing. Who will you interview next?

Glossary

information (in-fur-MAY-shuhn) knowledge and facts

interview (IN-tur-vyoo) a meeting during which a person is asked questions about herself or a subject

interviewee (in-tur-vyoo-EE) a person who is being asked questions about herself or a subject

opinion (uh-PIN-yuhn) a person's beliefs and ideas about somebody or something

paragraphs (PAIR-uh-grafss) groups of sentences about certain ideas or subjects

quotes (KWOHTSS) someone's exact words that are copied somewhere, such as in a piece of writing

recorder (rih-KOR-dur) a machine that copies sounds so they can be listened to later

research (REE-surch) careful study of something to learn about it

topic (TOP-ik) the subject of a piece of writing

For More Information

BOOKS

Jarnow, Jill. *Writing to Retell*. New York: PowerKids Press, 2006.

Raczka, Bob. *The Vermeer Interviews: Conversations with Seven Works of Art*. Minneapolis: Millbrook Press, 2009.

WEB SITES

BBC—Listening—Asking Questions
www.bbc.co.uk/schools/ks3bitesize/english/speaking_listening/listening/revise3.shtml
Look here to learn more about listening and asking questions.

Scholastic—How to Conduct an Interview
www2.scholastic.com/browse/article.jsp?id=3752516
Find more tips for conducting a great interview.

Index

About the Authors

Cecilia Minden, PhD, is the former Director of the Language and Literacy Program at Harvard Graduate School of Education. While at Harvard, Dr. Minden taught several writing courses for teachers. She is now a full-time literacy consultant and the author of more than 100 books for children. Dr. Minden lives in Chapel Hill, North Carolina, with her husband, Dave Cupp, and a cute but spoiled Yorkie named Kenzie.

Kate Roth has a doctorate from Harvard University in Language and Literacy and a masters from Columbia University Teachers College in Curriculum and Teaching. Her work focuses on writing instruction in the primary grades. She has taught first grade, kindergarten, and Reading Recovery. She has also instructed hundreds of teachers from around the world in early literacy practices. She lives in Shanghai, China, with her husband and three children, ages 2, 6, and 9. They do a lot of writing to stay in touch with friends and family and record their experiences.